on Women artists:

poems 1975-1980

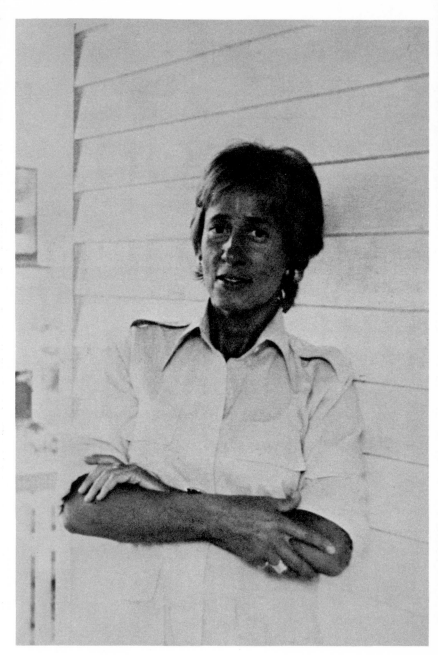

Alexandra Grilikhes   *Photograph: P.R. DePuy*

on Women artists:

poems 1975-1980

Alexandra Grilikhes

Sculpture and fiber art by Jean Van Harlingen

First Edition
First Printing: September 1981.

Library of Congress Catalogue Card Number:
    81-65430
ISBN: 0-939416-00-X

Photographs of the sculpture and fiber art by Jean Van Harlingen taken by the artist.

Design and Production by "3 sisters"
Cover Design by Jennifer Klein
Edited by Felice Newman

Published by Cleis Press
Printed in the United States

Some of these poems originally appeared in the following publications: *The WXPN Express, 13th Moon, Feminist Studies, Focus/Midwest, Film Library Quarterly, Occurrence, Poets on Photography, Contemporary Quarterly, Cameos: 12 Small Press Women Poets* (The Crossing Press, 1978). A portion of the prose also originally appeared in *Cameos*.

Grateful acknowledgement is made to the publishers of the following books from which some prose passages have been quoted: Originals: *American Women Artists* by Eleanor Munro (Simon and Schuster, 1979), *Dawns and Dusks* by Louise Nevelson (Charles Schribners and Sons, 1976), and *Theme for Diverse Instruments* by Jane Rule (Talonbooks, 1975).

For Blanche, My Mother,
The First Woman Artist I Knew

Contents

one

two

three

INTRODUCTION

I have been deeply influenced by other women artists who have worked in many forms. Their lives, their ways of being in the world, of perceiving, have given me both spirit and bread, and the impulse to go on with my own work.

This book is devoted to, is about, and is inspired by the work of other women with whom I have a great, a sympathetic kinship. I feel I am a part of an awesome and sacred tradition.

The poems in Part One invoke the spirit of the woman artist. In Part Two, the poems celebrate particular artists who have strongly affected me, women I have met in and through their art. Part Three contains poems in which I explore my own artistic process. Through that exploration I find the work I have done is what I am, as in dreams.

Alexandra Grilikhes

one

Back To Nature. A site piece constructed November 1980, Spring City, Pennsylvania. Plaster, fiber, cast paper. 30″ × 48″ × 36″, 36″ × 60″ × 36″, 24″ × 60″ × 30″.

I work from deep sources, trying to find a plumb line to drop myself down directly to that place.

In threading my way, I find that the act of creation is very much like what the Mistress of the Animals does.

The Great Mother was the oldest deity, then came the Mistress of the Animals, in reality, another version of the Great Mother.

Why it was that early folk felt and named the Great Mother is obvious, but for me, the Mistress of the Animals, one of people's earliest projections, is a more interesting figure because she is not really necessary. Her function is entirely symbolic. At a time when people were learning to live together, to subdue their wild animal selves in order to form society and ensure that it continue, they constructed a "Mistress of the Animals" in whose control they wanted to place their deep and ruthless feelings. That this controlling force had to be female is of both necessity and great beauty. People understood that they had to learn to live with their animal, to come to terms with it in order to survive.

I was enormously attracted by the idea that it is a female being who is strong enough to master all animal impulse, inner and outer. Throughout the history of art, she is there, shown as strong and female, surrounded by animals, grasping a beast in each arm or hand. The animals with her are usually described as "guarding her" but it is quite clear that it is she who is controlling them. That this power is female seemed not only true but *felt*. I mean felt as female by me, as I have never experienced the power of a male deity.

How then is the making of art analogous to what the great goddess does? To give coherence to the animal, inner and outer, is to transform, and at least on one level, to master.

Having found the *Potnia Theron* (as the Mistress is known in Greek) to be one of the deepest sources of my work (she has always leaped out at me from pages where she lies hidden or not so hidden) I searched deeper into my female consciousness, my own myth/history to locate my thoughts and feelings in the larger female consciousness. I experienced personal female deities, actually parts of myself, as modes of being to which I could turn in moments of desperation. Solitude is one of these. I know that if I do not lose my sense of connection to my female feelings I can be at one with myself no matter what is happening around me. This is often very difficult.

The deepest source of my work, my speechless animal, is not only alive but crucial to my ability to make art. The Mistress is both the animal and, because she has compassion, the animal's mother. She heals/I have to heal my wounded animal in order to live. All the transformative powers of this goddess reside in me; it is my choice and my need to use them well.

POTTER

Between
>   night and dark
>   nearness and far
>   sweetness and death

between sweetness and
>   death
>   nearness and
>   far

>   night and dark

her blue hands carry the great earth
cover, cut the spine of the wind

between
>   moisture and deep
>   the throat of the clay
voice

closes

>   hands   soft in the water
>   slow in the water
>   blurred hands   I

shall be drawn through

curve the spine of the wind
I shall be drawn through in magic
I shall be drawn through in
fever
>   open my hands in the
sea

>   enter the house

FEELING THE GODDESS   I

naked wood
caught between stones
one side smooth
the other seamoss —
covered, curved, splendid,
full of power. Surprised

I think of wild sea
prows curving, cracked by storms

      Scylla/Charybdis, you
said once, smiling. I have stopped
hearing the ceaseless
bell of the archipelago
rung by wind to warn
travelers. Circean

it rocks, lulls, draws, whispers
gently into wind begins
over be
warned of small
islands if you are a
traveler they are peaceful,
isolated, more
dangerous than they look

      Clarity of self of
place. Rocks
struck by lightning as I have
intuition.

Lying back I see
nothing. Trees. Blue pines. Crags.
Heat rising in ecstasy the
earth deserted today
for the last time. I
have abandoned everything except
isolation and some harmony
that waits for me after the cataclysm

but I don't race
towards the easy
life. As I knew
she would be there she
rises at my left
full of weeds and
water

I
know
her
she
drops
away
quick she was not
quick enough

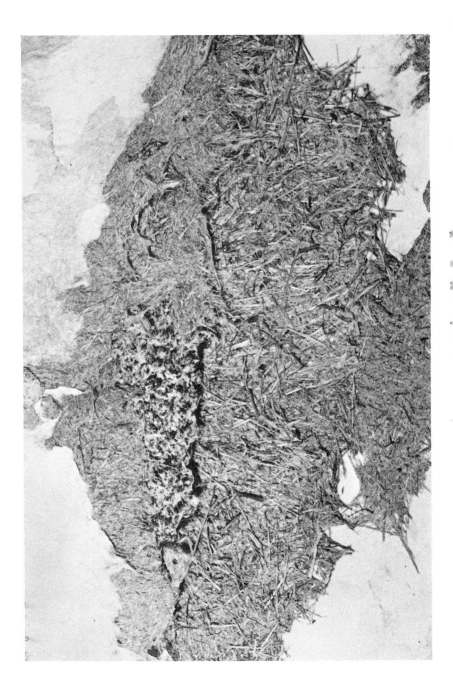

PROLOGUE

stranger you have
drifted to me
without sun without
wind without storm
my house a land
mark which holds
me where day after
day I wait for the
light and the dark
well the word *Xaipe*
spells in her breast.
I do not know
how I became stranger and
known, not hearing the
voices of journeys
that drive me, desire
for what I will be or
where go, not
the noises of hatred,
revenge. Stranger
I travel without sun
without wind my house
shipboard which rocks
me which opens
and keeps there the
face of Medusa
and loves her.

PHOTOGRAPHER

for J.R.

twilight
her camera moves across
water stones seagarbage
becomes baroque
magnificent underneath
nostrils the hands flaring strike shake,
steady the metal

       and terror-struck
       the fingers burn
       like matches
       warmth that brings forth
       shoots forth
       brings out
       buries
Demons. Hold still the machine that
shivers.

over the world of the bridge
the empty lots the
long journey
towards where
like a hand, tentative, that
draws
back as it moves
forward the camera
inexorable
touches

everything she
sees makes it
moveable
sees deep
lives
on its edge
tries to escape
endures it.

pieces. the bits of the film
welded together wrong in the order
right in her
movement hands
open fingers
wide always the mystery
of the others imagination the
pleasure of

WATCHING THE DANCE

for Martha Graham

the battle before us. Walk through
enthralled. From the spine
outwards, imitate the tree.

Where is the
leap from the maze? Always
the maze with bodies the
net wrapping up.

Brought to their knees.
Undulate. Pass
into afternoon. Unravel
the word that waits to be
formed in the mouth

             body
          in midair
breaks out in the instant
of wildness

         Who
       shrouds herself
with a quick shift
in the dark cloak upwards?
Imitate the tree. Words, the
body that's drawn from air
by the movement of will   iron
                          clad
                          moves

in the limbs
like the lioness
passes through grass
lands in sleep. Hands

shudder. Speaking. Force
air against mouth the arrogant
question. I
see them through
        fire the shimmering
faces fade in my face
the mouth feels the curve
of their limbs and I open them
slowly feeling serenely excited
closer and warmer
                    keeping my distance.
Here in the orchestra, there
on the stage, breaking
the flesh of the contract, my
love.

THE FILM BY THE WOMAN

No warning   she is
tormenting the
myth that torments

   you

struggle in the ravaged sky
the storm too large

wounded
where you least wish to be
wounded

where will you go with it?
It has always been yours
the death
or the mother

     it will be yours
more and more

THE VANGUARD ARTIST
DREAMS HER WORK

those
where our mouths
clasp and we're
overcome me continually
in the midst of important
matters

      Off in the Caribbean sky
      I'm taking a breath
      taking dive over the beautiful
      cliff and the
flower soaks through me I
fantasize terrific
longings in color
      spending it all you
      become fruit in my
veins soaking through soaking
through I
hit water
swimming for life

I have always known myself as different from other people. Being an artist was an important part of that.

Unless there is someone out there who gives you a signal that it is possible for you to work as an artist, that it is a serious matter, that it has meaning, you may be lost. You do this for others when you get the chance, even if no one did it for you.

When I was twenty I took home to my father my first published poem. "Ah," he cried, holding it up, "my name in print!" It took me years to understand what he was saying although I became immediately angry.

These selected texts/quotes to which others could be added are a progressive means of self-identification. My name with the work attached. A small dam against isolation. A black ribbon of print on the page, permeable, through which flows my whole past, my father, his name, the things I choke on even now.

The opacity of the dam, the utter opacity of the future. The battle to keep oneself swelling into being, away from the annihilation of self, a self that depends too much on others and on what will be said of one. The vertigo of turning these feelings, raw and alive, into words.

two

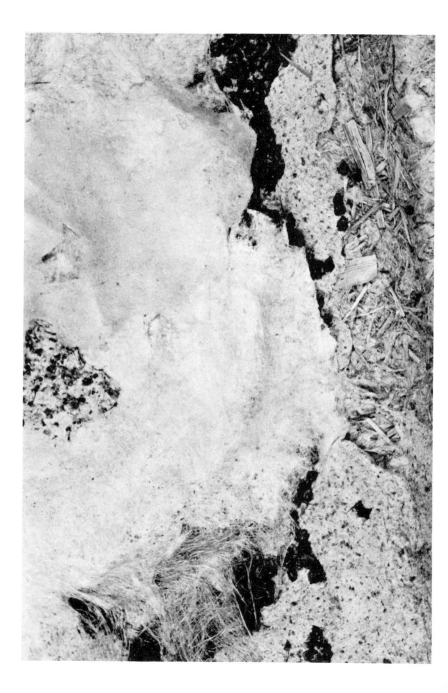

There are times when I can't work, can't do anything.
I can't concentrate, I get scattered, feel I'm dying.
                                    — Mary Frank

When I'm unable to work I seek succor in their work.
If my writing is a gagged stream, theirs is not. Their
work moves into mine and so suggests to me that
mine is available to me, somewhere in me.

Reading another woman's work, looking at her art;
spirit and bread. Passion. It's what I live for, the
beautiful alive, the reality that passes between us,
something that makes me live, a kind of nurturing.
The elements lie inert in me ready to burn on
contact. A laval heat.

The animal, separated from the jungle dreams of
burying herself in the sun. She weeps and starts in
her dream, shudders. Wakened by her own noise, she
growls, then roars, a melted down magma that is
intelligible to me as the words I repeat somewhere in
my deepest hurts and rages.

I dream of a whole word which contains the frag-
ments of my self. It waits at the edge of language,
always.

———————

17

I who live daily close to madness and its wily justifi-cations love too much to go there and I cannot stand anyone else taking an energy ride out of that perverse imagination. But I don't want my power to cut out, I wanted to go away, to live in myself, unoffending, somewhere else.

— Jane Rule

The repeated movement; the standing before and the standing before the canvas, the sitting down, the drawing forward of the chair and the sitting down, the sitting down at the table before the typewriter before the paper, the space of the dance studio, the repetition as if in a film, the constant "before me" of the work, a continual beginning, beginning the dance.

———————

SPEED THE SLOW UP: VIOLA FARBER

American dancer-choreographer.

                To
you
of all people
I wanted to be opaque
throw my hands into the glass

image of my resurrection

              all I want
a lingering opacity

            movement   silences
           moments and silences

                I want to leave in you
                the aura that is mine
always to   reveal you   reveal you   reveal you

the glass
      walls
        gesture
          timestretch
stretch it is a solid rage that engorges
far beyond you your beats
nothing you could see
feel by the squeak of my
bare feet my
body wrenched up
tight into itself

first   NOT THE SLAP
                of hands against thighs the
                wack of feet think
                of someone who committed
                suicide what rage
                your body conjures

face flushed your hands
bulging on the seat the
savage endings of your body's
      wish for wish
for wish for me   the raged
innocence   longings that know bounds that
go on spending, circle, take the path, prepare
the last confluence of the limbs
                          drive the body
drop
  you close your eyes
  push me out of you

Watch her. The times you have pulled back in life
before you've reached the end. She reaches the end.

SIMONE SIGNORET TALKING OF LANGLOIS
IN TRUFFAUT'S FILM, "HENRI LANGLOIS"

Simone Signoret, contemporary French film actress.

harden? soften? shatter? blur? go
down? Her
face
struck
down by the
flashings of our
intentions   lightly she fingers

shadows underneath her eyes, touches
on Langlois slowly, "I am old,

and I remember him very well."

the better to feel
with her nails are
short her flesh
has felt   much the inner
                            confusions
                            not
                            having
                            the right
                            words, the hands
move, Langlois
during the war and the years

              Remembering him
aloud blowing
smoke her hands describe her life's
curves a thousand ways,
telling you this,
that, all
the time talking of him, how

a woman touches off

so much without your having
asked how
in the middle of telling
you something else.

POET

*for Marina Tsvetaeva, Russian
poet of tremendous talent
whose life, lived as an out-
sider, culminated in her suicide
at age 48.*

first invocation

a heavy smoker
you only had a corner
of the room. They hated
smoke.

You had to go outside
into the freezing calm
between translating
Peter Pan
and deep
exhaling;

Smoke

poured

Frenzy. Stones and rotting.
Furies. Words the
words !

23

second invocation

to smoke
you had to go
outside into the winter, emptiness,
the
sky your
violent gaze, still
empty still
the poems;

      figures slammed into the
sea where there is suddenly
light in your blood
one image floods the
other through the
cold, the
smoke, your
eyes, your
life

your life

third invocation

a heavy smoker

you had a corner
in the room. The other
people, strangers, hated
smoke. You had to go outside
into the frozen
calm of Russia through the smoke
turbulence

        images
        one upon the other
        running in your
        skull like heat

delirium of hands
of head of weather

        all there was.

PHOTOS FROM BLONDEAU

Barbara Blondeau, Photographer
1938-1974

the door opens

cracks the street of
alchemy no
map

   when you speak of it they
know it well the
word pierces their
mouths

    the
way the eye ascends
one hand over the moon

out of the fingertips
writhing of islands
underground streams
glaciers visibly melting a
plethora/
      /bodies in motion
split by the will of the
watcher waiting the moment
to black them in daylight

               The
dross of this world burns
your poverty is inescapable your
hands open

you're falling

to the place of return the
purity of that which is hidden
visible things emptied
pure in the light turned to glass
she was pitiless. It is simple
to say she was animated
by her art made curious by vision
the passion that drove
her the
dross burns
Off

        they race forward in glass,
shift, flaunt themselves
at your face flip their shoulders
multiply and are gone

he had two of them in his house two
of her photos the rest were elsewhere

what she saw you did not see what she made
you did not make you can say you knew her
you did not

willed shuttered the strobe
lights she
was animated you might say forced forward
by her art not the muse the duende not
the dust the earth not the earth the
mother

I feel myself
forced forward by her
hands the sky
opens

in which I am alone
wanting to return, turn
back, swimming to flay
distance, eyes
unseeing to lie
quiet on the black green frame
of her life till
one of us splits open

she waited she
knew she would
die this is the
miracle

MOIRA

for my sister N., painter

the message
rests   the
music is late my
body thinks itself
into the lines on my
palm I remember her
accent her story of
journeys my fear

then the sojourn in madness
where no one spoke except
it caused pain and my own
pain crept out of my mouth.
Speechless I tossed

in the net of the forest
or the bottom of the sea
where even the fish swam
with their eyes turned away

Under a sky made of lead
I opened the package: a brilliant
blue shirt and your words,
          "remember your moira."

I rose
and my
hands and my
journeys
rose with me
past the rhythm of death
seeing your colors,
clay, green, blue, Euclid
your mentor the
unknown Graces your
mystery.

      Clear on a death day
my spirit lay empty
the floor of my life, "remember
your moira." Remind me as
I shall remind you.

NEVELSON

Louise Nevelson, American sculptor, now in her 80's.

We are in a dark place.
The joists pull us into and
upward past the barriers of
time that gray us as we stand
outside the window of skin,
watch for the sun to fall, set, become
intenser, blind us, fade. They pass us
who watch noisy and go on toward afternoon.
But this place means darkness, sun,
and a timeless conflagration of
all our love and watchfulness. We
cannot move into this carpentry, it
moves into us, climbs our joists and
hollows, forever follows our fingers.

JOAN SUTHERLAND

*brilliant Australian-born coloratura soprano
frequently referred to as "La Stupenda".*

You are in the light.

The nimbus of your power breaks
loose, furls, unfurls, surrounds
your body which is tight, straight,
full, the vessel for your voice that
makes you larger than my life or theirs.

I curve the gestures of your silent hands
a dumbshow in my bones. You
spend your warmth, the discipline
that burns us with the blunt
points of its entering force.

Merciless, the lights bare you, brave,
gold, in the glare of gazes and your passion,
the tormented eyebrows, the
prison of your stance, your hands and
feet severely motionless, you sing.
Afterwards a deep breath, a moment
off the tightrope. You are not us. We
carry off what we could not give, get
somehow to you. Our mouths are fierce
with shouting as we wildly clap, the
strain between us taut. Yes,
we are alive a moment, stunned and
burned, and small, too small for this.

RAINFOREST

for Carolyn Brown, for many
years the leading dancer of the
Merce Cunningham Company.
Now a choreographer teacher
on her own.

for the furious

hairflying woman
even the silvered helium moves
in its black magic
takes the blame, the
zones whisper, the air
turns to squall, she,
lioness. Forests
shudder, pressing earthquakes
together for
her.
    Rain
    huges like tidal
    seas

    it doesn't
move it poises dead
still her body blazes I
burst into tears

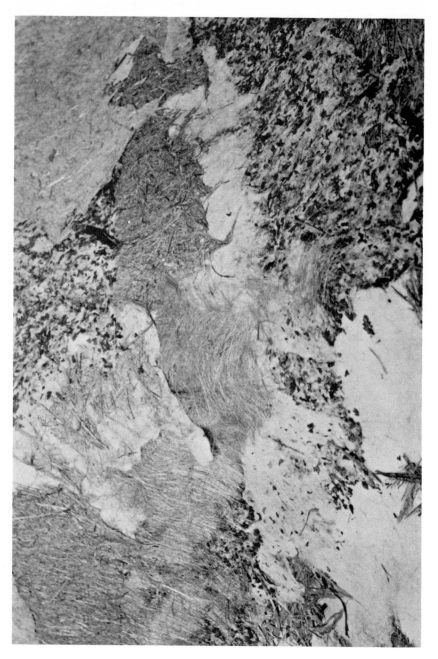

Nature's Process Reclaimed II. Detail.

MARGUERITE DURAS: AN HOMAGE

originator of the French "New Wave" in films.
Novelist, scenarist, film director, essayist.

no one goes into the forest

           I listen to the dogs

           the doors creaking

           until I get dizzy

sometimes I hear my own voice

           how excited I can get at night

I hear the dogs in the distance

           Who would believe the nights

           are so painful when it is so calm

there's the forest
it's dangerous

           I look at it and see it, that's how I know

           it's dangerous because I am afraid of it

Every night
I start writing a book I don't write

           Do you go into the forest?

           Not alone, no.

there is a gliding from Elisabeth to Alissa.
for a few seconds they are one and the same.
this can be called love.

Will you come into the forest?

           you're afraid of me

    it   take   in the forest

    Let's   the walk

    was   *I miss her*

    her gait

When she says I sleep I see her sleeping I see you
watching her sleep

because of what you've been through
                        things happen to you
                  that have never happened before

He saw Alissa as continually seesawing between life
and death

she belongs to whoever wants her
she feels whatever the other one feels
she would have gone into the forest with Alissa
                              Asleep. Our kind of
                        Sleep.

Alissa: the one who
destroys and brings on madness in all its power
        She's dreaming destruction, the loud noises
        she can't direct her own dreams
or her power   to pass from numbness
                              to wake

it's coming from the forest. How difficult it is. It
must force its way through everything.

She had used a certain emptiness in herself as a
starting point

                              she wanted to go away
                                    alone

she toyed with the idea of taking some step
to change things and as time passed she felt the
situation less and less tolerable. She had to do
something

> there's a heavy cement block
> inside her

walking home on a late spring night they talked
of scuba diving. She could see the green moss
and blue plants that flicker near the ocean floor.

At five o'clock in the morning she wakens. She loves
the mystery in the eyes. They're impenetrable. She
turns on her other side. It's five twenty-five. The
eyes again. Opaque. She wanted to look into them

she heard the words, "loneliness is a trick"

Desire for anesthesia

she awakened with severe intermittent claudication
in her left calf. She cried out in pain.

"The only thing that will have ever happened to
you," she says, "is you," Elisabeth says, "You,
Alissa."

she tried to think of a reward at the
end of her mind that would be without pain

There were few material possessions in her house but
each was beautiful and carefully chosen

It is the dark stone
in which your face shows
I felt you moving towards me

It's fascinating to see the way you live," she
says, "fascinating and terrible !"

years later she will dream of the Gorge and the sun
losing its light

as she waited

MESHES OF THE AFTERNOON

*for Maya Deren, American avant garde
filmmaker of the 40's and early 50's
who died at the age of 44.*

three selves
about the table
about the table

the knife in the bread
falls

the dream
opens her memory
opens her memory   the knife
                              twists
on the pillow beside her
her eyes close she
follows the figure that
strides with the face made of glass
she follows
her she can never
catch up she will
follow

the three selves
the face made of mask

she ascends
on the stairs she is
moved by the
squall of her nightmare
moved and the seaweed or is it the
cord of the telephone
trembles ?

Like this one,
all of her deaths,
her last one,
lives.

ON SEEING A FILM BY BETTE GORDON, 1980

American vanguard filmmaker.

She moves past the first

set of doors with a purposeful
stride as if she is going somewhere

longitudinal cracks from chipped paint
greet her there is a rhythm there is a
certain dance that matches the legs
that are moving I heard your voice
saying making love is, I know, for
you, like a dance

Coming up the railroad tracks in the snow
I watched her figure moving from
side to side plodding, enjoying the movement
of crunching the snow I love that
figure as the woman in the frame
who seems to come no closer draws closer
yet in my mind only, recedes

Again I see tracks in the snow
with no figure just the tracks
in the distance and the sun continues to
set no woman coming towards me

The process of moving forward and at the
same time backward going round the corner
and yet not going can be felt here where
your eye does it you are not part of this
except that body there that long brown hair
the perspiration are yours the pursed
lips the flowing cloth

You're connected
        as if with wires

three

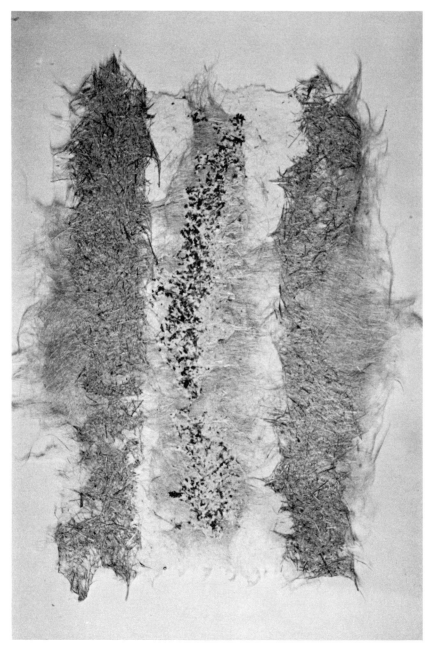

Strata   Wall Hanging   9" × 13"   Natural Fibers and Dies

APPROACHING

for Annette Michelson

I

three things he said
were important to me then
consciousness
resonance
stillness

all I want she said
not stillness
quiet

sometimes I said
I thought I had stillness
then I find I don't
so I removed my watch

he said
I no longer look for those
three

I thought:
to be resonant

II

he said
how do you live
if not like that ?

By wanting
to lose myself
in something
it's what I live for

Wanting to lose
yourself, he said,
in something ?

PRAYER TO MY EMBLEMS

"Going on is the enormous thing I do."
—Hanne Darboven, German artist whose style
focuses on the repetition of mathematical
work.

       hung on the
wall by the threads of sense.
Orange and solace. Deep
yellow. Full of gold
myths and tempers, symbols of
Minos and my journeys called
"Cretan Memory One." Metaphors

of the body
it moves too from the wall
towards me where I
move in and out of its
plays emblazoned by
fixtures and
sounds it is all
inner and outer
as in the past they do everything
differently. Movement. Always
alive. I have been trying to
say I love this afternoon
translucent as it slips into evening
blasting with horns and
sounds that pass my limits
into the walls of my life
and my room. The
smoke of my voice
dips into itself and

dies. I am poised
on the horns of Minos. Front and
center the cup curved of clay
flowers has nothing inside it.
Then horns. Above, a
vessel that pours
water suspended in air on a fall
evening where twice
I have looked
into my hands for trophies
and found that my
hands are my trophies.

       You
in the evening
pass me and color
everything in the room.
Into the voyage that
fades, blisters, goes
and comes back, your
face as if veiled beneath
water then mirrored. Both seem
true as I gaze into royalty
I've given you, drown
a little, let my senses
blur into my blazons, backdrop,
talisman, signal of the
source of my moorings. I have made
this out of nothing the
sun and the goddess
worked through my hands
I'm grateful for that. All
the shadows I live for swing

out into the room strike hard
as I move down the street, stunned,
solitary, locked into the faults
of my feeling, feeling
my dry mouth dry. A

blazon of hand-movements, color,
Cretan memory one, coping stone
of the myth   I am alive in
and my hopes rise, longing for that
place where the sea anemones
grow that is hidden, impossible to
find without being led there.
And if it is love that drives me to
move in the world then I am driven,
drive to the soundings of music that
break through the walls. As I
never have
          I go into the dance
and I leave it, come back, loving the
evening, pushed as it is in opposite
directions; It is the extremes that
touch me, recoil and start back;
Going on
in the enormous thing I do.

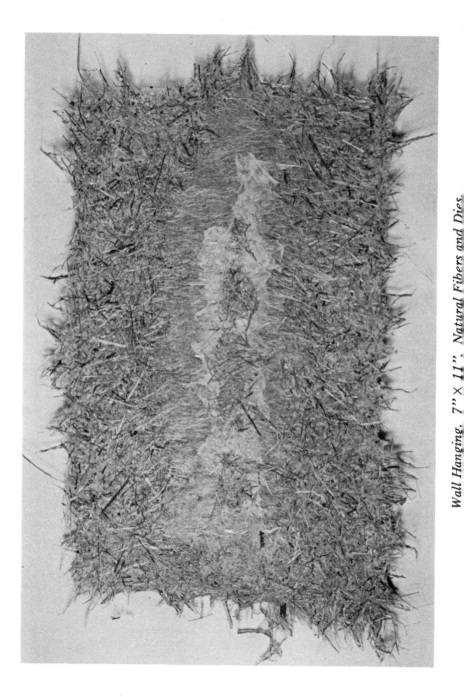

Wall Hanging. 7" × 11". Natural Fibers and Dies.

DARKROOM: THE STRANGER

over her shoulder I see
her fingers burning
and dodging me in and
remember

      droplets of ocean
oars turning in water.
She moves past me

in the yellow light our
heads bent watching her

the wars inside me,
strange, a languid
tone a
look faraway I
want to
spear you
into my wits there is nothing
I can do can you do the
stranger who says I love you

torpor, the
white
space, winter.   Winter

the heartbeat that changes to
music. I push back and
forth the
plants on the
shelf thinking,   "small",   "citydweller's".

and one truth only cuts the dull glass
window and if I'm lucky today drives me.
Rooting a cut of mint
in the blue metal
pot. Her
shaded face.

THE WHITE POEMS

*"I wish the idea of time would
drain out of my cells and leave me
quiet even on this shore."*
*—Agnes Martin, American painter now in
her 70's who lives and works in the
New Mexico desert.*

1. PLACE.

the form is wood
though it is sometimes water

a white wall
everything to be changed
the mind changed   the
time of day. Begin
very early the light
trembling, immaculate and
soft

circle round it
raise the wood of the
table to your
hand move down to it
and write becoming
one with wood

what floats
in the mind
in the sea-mirror
everything in the wood

Image: the color of fruit, bitter and
yellow, the wood will merge
with you under your hand
with you without words
you rise later, released,
part of a stream of blood that's
unnameable that's not yours
any longer

can you gain time
as you slip back

into the memories that
grasp you ?

The white poem; the moment
the hands come together
holding something, putting it
down, the pall of dailiness
goes

  It is morning. The white
poem moves into place.

2. SOUNDDANCE

Begins in the nerve. The body remains
still begins to spell
its pulse on the wall

the mirror's
flash as the
impulse carries itself out

        Inexorable
like the eyes
of a deaf person maneouvering
around you
to see your lips
breaking
and coming
together

3. SOLO

The impulse that
shouts begins
in the brain

in the fluorescent
light of the evening
the body turns on itself
slowly, spirals
out of itself, breaks out
of its frame, there's
always
the need
to break out of the
frame once you have found it

throw yourself into the air arms
upflung, come down very
                              slowly

are seen against
white which
picks up the
impulse like radar. Carve

beasts of stone on the walls of the cave
Over and over the mysteries
repeat themselves
we turn them we
hold them we
spread them before us

the table of
wood the
room without furniture
the walls white.
Solitude. A neighbor who.
The part of the city where few people live.

You're sitting alone by the open window
the sky is white though it's evening. A
young fearless girl stretches her limbs
in you, leaps, stares ahead at the open
field, begins to run until she is
breathless. She is
you. You are breathless.
The torn photograph
makes a beautiful negative though it is
thirty years old. Your
hand photographed as you now
hold the photograph in your hand. Your hand.
Your hand that makes everything. Your
hands. Give me your hands.

4. RUNE

Old photos. The early
movements bared, decipherable,
the eyes as if seen
for the first time.
The language of
leanings or twistings
away.

You.

The old dance. the slow
enchainements. the brown
image grows till it
fills the
space/space
that is no
space. Sometimes
a lovely dance.

the photographs a
way to dig yourself
in. Rare
metal.

    Base metal. The
curve of the
imagination caught in the
brilliant physical undertow

flow of water falling and
gushing in streams. Waking
as if in a dream of light.
Heavy steps. The
one who was changed.

You are outside
time and every word is a
movement you cannot control. The
dense planes of the trees
plane upon plane a
figure moves in and out of the
landscape like consciousness. A
Giorgione landscape.

Over and over in our lives
the mysteries contain us
repeat themselves

5. *TORSE*

for J.H.

The afternoon
begins with the idea of the blue
cyanotype. A network of muscle
your hands and shoulders deep
shadow to white your
eyes brilliant, intent

on the calculus of the
journey the one taken then
the one taken now

only one at the mercy of journeys
is drawn into their purpose

you wrote on the cloth, "my
feet meet the pacific ocean."

you open the door your
eyes and I'm overcome seeing past
you, you, washing the prints
while you're lit in the naked
yellow of the darkroom bulb

my voice in a letter to myself,
harsh words of a stranger,

"do not allow yourself the comfort
of repeating your strategies."

Across the room Brad's blue shirt
becomes the blue cyanotype squares
printed on muslin we've spread
on the floor: a graph, a path,
blockage, meaning I wanted to find.
The other pleasures,

those of pain, terror, the
extremes that drive you the
welcome extremes without which

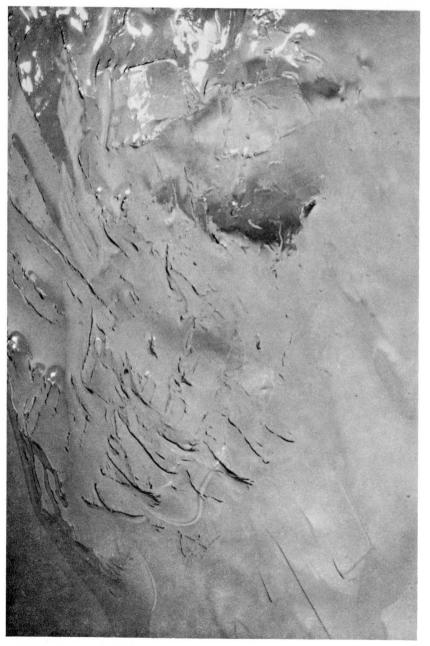

Vision of a Sculptor's Efforts. Detail.

6. SIGNALS

for B.C.

in the fluorescent light of the evening
you strike Maine for me and I feel *there*
in the granite, the gorge, swimming
and holding my breath till I
rise for a moment for air
then return to that world

morning stretches out of the sea
and I rise with it having lain empty and
dead in the night, the
island belongs to the morning where
it ends on the stones in the stream of my life

I write on the board, "don't allow
yourself the comfort of repeating your
strategies. Don't be satisfied. Don't
protect yourself."

                    I want to take off my
sweater and feel the freezing
air on my shoulders, push past my
life the slow
motions of
desire not
taken the
slow

motions of power in water the
strong entry the tropical
sea

   across the room
   Brad's blue shirt
   becomes the blue cyanotype
   square in the hands
   on the floor

   in the house the sunlight
   blurred, soft through the
   plastic that's over the
   windows

Disgorging my thought which leaves me
electric   I do nothing with it
but feel.

7. TRAVELOGUE

for J.H.

my voice in a letter
harsh words of a stranger,
"do not allow yourself the comfort
of repeating."

I think of you
I think of warmth
I think of your life
system putting forth
branches in all directions

In your kitchen we talk. It is very
cold. During the days that follow
I think of warmth. It corrodes my whole
system as I walk down the street

When I meet you again
I become your eyes
seeing at once my silence

the white poem enchains
the thought of the white poem enchains

8. SOUNDWAVE

the feedback fed
back. I wake up early. The
white poem moves into
place. The
loneliness
of the white
morning, explosion of
consciousness, the
edge of the sea
inside your body

      the eye
      lid with the thick
      lash shudders down
      slowly
It was a door that opened to me
once. The whitewashed walls, the
names of Crete, the passage
into my veins   where I came
from   where I stayed
There.

I test the floor with a few quick
slides. I walk to the window
of the studio, trace
the glyph
and it is never visible even in dust.

the
door that
opens, the
power to assume a
shape, the
danger of the transformation and
wildness of the pleasure. A
voice of memory breaks the dream, the
      stronger than the voice that
holds you, blind.

            I
     twist in my
     seat driven
     along with my
secret/ the trees grow
darker. Words left
sharpening my
throat, throttle. I'm
excited with   terror
sustained by fantasy the
one redemption in this car ride;
the obsessive secret
     sustains,
always sustains.

9. REBUS

for Maya Deren

the eye
lid like a
shutter
closes down
slowly

the screen
darkens we
know we are/
             she is
dreaming

the key becomes
knife, the
knife key, she
takes the key
from her mouth
her eyes charged and
dark
strides through each element
holding the knife

            first the foot
            then the fist
            with the knife

then the foot
then the fist
with the knife

my choice and my will

this energy circles the body
like flame

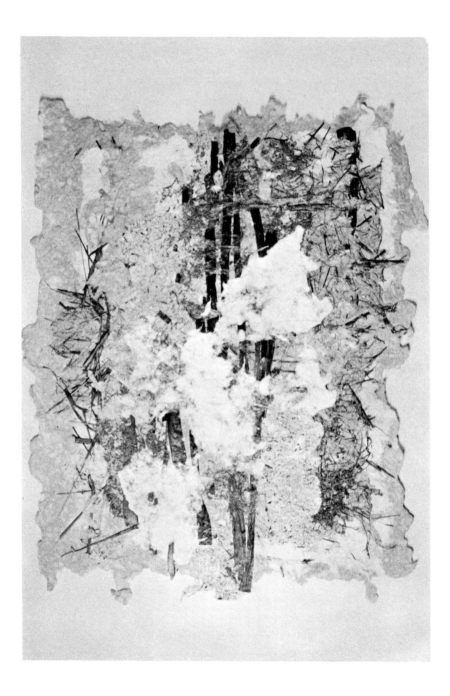

CHOKED ON THE BEGINNINGS

choked on the beginnings
yes
successes flail
in the throats of the others. Loss
treats. The songs of
triumph finish me even here

where there are no
questings no
finishings. Work.
It is all
simple. Recollections. Fantasy of
excellences, applause of
planets. My work, finished
before the beginning

weeds up
out of the dark, flowers
indiscriminate, culminates with
thorns in my successful mouth. Lying
dreaming I do my work, leave it
prone in the dark
with me. My
work is to dream only.

MEDUSA, SMILING

I.

To you
great lady
I dedicate the storm
ing flower
writhing in my wits while
brazen pride and
fear, bronze
in all their harshness
move and move
in the tomb
of my hands for you Medusa
always for you

> oh when
> was it
> that the eyes
> of the sun
> were on me
> and I turned
> gold on the branch
> my tongue singing
> praises other than these ?

Fond
mother, stone
mother, with me now
in weariness, in
dark
water I see you now Medusa
see your face at last
with my face
in your eyes, gleaming.

". . . particularly for the woman artist, the Muse is
nothing but Medusa turned backwards. You face the
implacable force in yourself with which you must
find how to live, Medusa, the terrible unknown that
one mines and one mines, and of whom the end never
comes. You use it rather than let it turn you to stone.
Medusa, for you if you choose; she isn't outside
you."

(from a letter written to May Sarton May 30, 1964)

II

May I hear at last
the last terrifying
jangle of the silent
musics, find it finally
and be victorious, look
on the last madness,
brilliance
of the secret
Medusa
deep into the eyes
find the last long terror-
stricken thing that
lies wound
and violent in the hidden self
and smile.

But what is our happiness? What does it mean to say
or think, "my happiness?" The only real one I know
is the process, not the result of working. The repeated
movement; the standing before and the standing
before the canvas. The sitting down, the drawing
forward of the chair, the sitting down, the sitting
down at the table before the typewriter, before the
paper, the dance, the repetition, as in a film, the
constant "before me" of the work, a continual
beginning, beginning the dance. The forgetting of
everything else.

I am closer to the work than to anything on earth.
That's the marriage. — Louise Nevelson

The picking up of the pieces. Making something.
The challenge. The game. The seriousness. The trance.
Happiness as never experienced by the presence of a
lover. Different from the position of wanting or
expecting something from someone. Working, you
aren't waiting for something that might never come.
You aren't waiting.

The mystery of one's work. The scene of forgetful-
ness, of total engagement without which life would
be an unblinking present in which there is no relief
from the glare of fluorescent lights, the punishment
and drudgery of dailiness, a job, an office, a desk,
those who patronise you, the politics of surviving in
a context in which you have no control, the life that
consumes the marrow of your bones until you are
drained, you cannot think or move or make anything.

I think of my nights. They were more despairing than
my days because at night I could not keep moving,
I had to come to a stop.

75

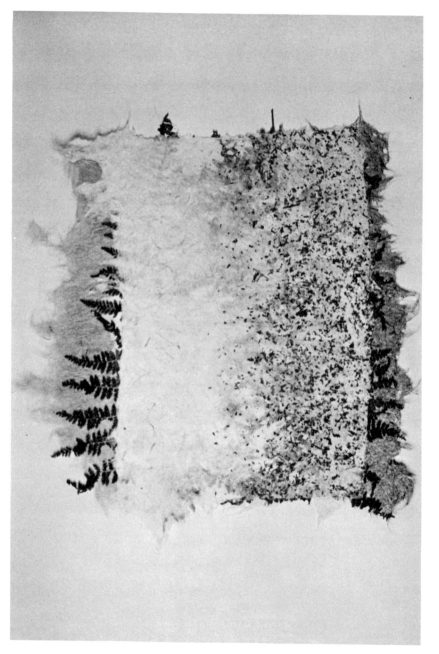

Above Timber Line. Wall Hanging. 14" x 14". Natural Fibers and Dies

CROSSROAD

1. Seaglass, beachglass,
windlass, a ship's
compass

how much you forget the
secrets of the sea
when you are away from them

the myth I want
is not the horse-god Poseidon
but the woman who, each year,
enters the water and marries the sea

Seawater and blood
they are the same weight they
fuse you become whole when the
sea enters your veins, not the sea
is divine but the spirit of the
sea it is what you enter

                        The tide
comes in the
boat is lifted and dragged
back when the tide is pulled
forward the boat is brought
out to the waves

                  memory,
you stretch past me as I lie
in your hammock, swinging

2. There are times
        I look into the mirror

and see the eyes of my grandmother,
sometimes the eyes of my father
they were not related I don't know whose
eyes these are

3. A long time ago I said " I
don't know whose hand this is, when
I look into the mirror I don't
know whose hand or whose face or whose eyes these
are"

4. Each day a different journey
opens in my palm. Sometimes their meanings
escape me. I find I've said the
wrong thing, touched the
wrong person, looked into the
wrong eyes.

5. I'm holding a small shell with a hole
bored in its center by a sea animal. I
look through it and see the world, surrounded
by the edge of a shell.

I could be anywhere, enclosed by
alabaster, a perfect, deeply ridged shell.

6. Behind my own voice, the words bleed through
like a second station on the radio:

> "you have my face, my
> bones, my sorrow, my
> loneliness. I will them to you."

The struggle. To desire, to know
light.

The poverty of dreams is sometimes unbearable. Then, an undertow between memory and forgetfulness, the unexpected abundance of dreams, where, sinking into a calm or storm I rise and lift into a life I want. The magnificent and fruitful gifts, the surprises of the dream. What I really want. Is this some form of the goddess, that primitive form again? My unconscious knows her well for she lies there like an animal, wanting, always wanting.

The part of myself located on the dark side, like moss, lies unseen, and always in the dark. Unable to write it down, something goes round in my head as if it is being carefully written down. Meanwhile, I am staring into space, riding the elevator.

I am in a restaurant where they announce the evening's dishes. Some of them are fish cooked in parchment and other things medieval. I am excited by that thought, medieval food, but I will not eat it.

The person in the room who is unnoticed, unneeded, can see that which is usually not seen.

Outside the walls of my sleep and my studio is the encroaching real world; rape, starvation, death, torture, the extremity I can't face. If I face it I will be unable to lift my hand to try to make art or to have a thought that is frivolous, or of the soul, but not "useful" or tormented, guilty or terrified. Mary Daly's book, *Gyn/Ecology*. I felt paralyzed by its truths. Susan Griffin's book *Women and Nature*. I could neither sleep, nor speak, nor go about my daily business. The horror. I look at the little dog and recall how I interact with her. What I expect without thought. She is submissive and obeys orders. She is faithful to her master above all others. She behaves appreciatively when given a treat. Hanging on your words and gestures, her life depends on you. She will receive the little punishments she knows of for infractions of the rules, for disobedience. I suddenly feel unable to interact with this dog and these thoughts too are paralyzing.

I am badly armed. I fight for concentration, for commitment, for honesty, constancy. I wait, and always realize, surviving until the early morning that I can't wait. I don't have time.

THE EMBRACE

Let the ordeal come down with me

Let the ordeal wait with me

Let the ordeal find me

Let the ordeal uproot me

Let the ordeal absorb my hatreds and

    let me accept them

Let it come down on me

Let the ordeal feel me in its fever

Let the ordeal crack me in its jaws

Twist me in its labyrinth

Find me in its tomb

Know me for desperate, no place to turn

Let the ordeal spit me out

over the trees

swing past the leaves and the branches

what is left of me

still able to feel after the numbness

On The Work of Jean Van Harlingen

The first piece of sculpture I saw by Jean Van
Harlingen, "Nature's Process Reclaimed," though on
a small scale, had a monumental quality. It is indeed
a mountainous piece, curving up and breaking the
surface of the earth, yet remaining a part of earth.

Jean works with and includes in her sculpture, as in
most of her work, the unaltered raw materials of
rough grown fiber. From these stalks and plants to
the finished paper we can see the whole process
embedded in the piece. All its possibilities are there,
from the totally raw stuff to the finished paper, a
sophisticated project, taken all the way to its end,
but never far from its earth-source.

Jean's wall hangings, made of natural fibers and dyes
have much the same feeling of nature in her process
of becoming. I love the primitiveness of the pieces.
They seem to come exactly from that place where my
own sources lie. Taking the raw material in its ele-
mental state she transforms it into art and doesn't
lose the feeling of the source. I, too, work from deep
sources, translating into language the raw material of
feeling, not to lose by language the purity and ele-
mental quality of my source. I too want to stay close
to her who gives me sustenance and is the source of
all things.

Alexandra Grilikhes

Alexandra Grilikhes has taught the Poet's Workshop
at the New Studies Center of the Philadelphia College
of the Performing Arts, and produced the only poetry
programs heard regularly in Philadelphia, during the
past eight years. She also teaches workshops in poetry
at the Women's School. She conceived and directed
Philadelphia's annual International Festivals of
Film By Women, and originated the "Woman
Poet" reading series in 1973. She has written broadly
on film, dance, and poetry, and her poetry has
appeared in many periodicals.

Other books by the same author include:

Isabel Rawsthorne Standing in a Street in Soho. N.Y.
Folder Editions, 1972.
Sea Agon. Providence, The Woodbine Press, 1976.
Body/With Words. Philadelphia, Atlantis Editions,
1976.
City Poems. Philadelphia, Moore College of Art Print-
making Department, 1977.
Landing On The Blue Plain. Birmingham, Ragnarok
Press, 1978

———————

Jean Van Harlingen was trained as a painter, sculptor
and papermaker. She works in fine arts, crafts and
performing arts. For more than fifteen years Jean has
made art connected to nature's own processes. Early
painting and performance works focus on textures,
movement, colors, and abstract landscapes. Early
sculptures abstractly capture movement in and through
a landscape, or conceptually connect to transparencies
and nature's multi-leveled depths.

Later sculptures are designed for particular outdoor environmental locations and speak to a number of political and social issues connected to our relationship to the earth as mother and provider. Recent works in paper are a natural outgrowth of nature's own processes of accumulation, assemblage and compression.

Jean has worked as an artist, art educator and artistic coordinator for public and private organizations and schools. She was coordinator for the Visual Artists in Public Service Program in Philadelphia from 1977-80. She has maintained her own studio in Philadelphia since 1975.